Guided **SCIENCE READERS**™

# Animal Stars

**SCHOLASTIC**

**GUIDED SCIENCE READERS™**

# Animal Stars

### by Timothy LeRoy

## SCHOLASTIC INC.

NEW YORK • TORONTO • LONDON • AUCKLAND • SYDNEY • MEXICO CITY • NEW DELHI • HONG KONG

Photographs © 2011: Alamy Images/Buddy Mays: 3; iStockphoto: 5 (Andrew Howe), cover & 1, (Eric Isselée), 7 (manley099), 6 (PhotoTalk); Photo Researchers, NY/Hans Reinhard: 8; Seapics.com/Doug Perrine: 4; ShutterStock, Inc./photobar: 2.

---

No part of this publication may be reproduced, stored in a retrieval system, or transmitted in any form or by any means, electronic, mechanical, photocopying, recording, or otherwise, without written permission of the publisher. For information regarding permission, write to Scholastic Inc., Attention: Permissions Department, 557 Broadway, New York, NY 10012.

ISBN 978-0-545-34810-2

Cover and interior design by Holly Grundon. Photo research by Jenna Addesso.

Copyright © 2011 by Lefty's Editorial Services. All rights reserved. Published by Scholastic Inc.
SCHOLASTIC, GUIDED SCIENCE READERS, and associated logos are trademarks and/or registered trademarks of Scholastic Inc.

25 24 23 22 21 20 19 18 17     24 25 26/0
Printed in China.     68

Fastest!

A cheetah is an animal star.
It is very fast!

A sloth is an animal star.
It is very slow!

Biggest!

A whale is an animal star.
It is very big!

A mouse is an animal star.
It is very small!

A rabbit is an animal star.
It is very soft!

A turtle is an animal star.
It is very hard!

A peacock is an animal star.
It is very beautiful! Wow!

**GUIDED SCIENCE READERS**

www.scholastic.com

**GUIDED SCIENCE READERS**™

**D**

# Chicken Life Cycle

**SCHOLASTIC**

**GUIDED SCIENCE READERS**™

# Chicken Life Cycle

**by Lydia Carlin**

## SCHOLASTIC INC.

NEW YORK • TORONTO • LONDON • AUCKLAND • SYDNEY • MEXICO CITY • NEW DELHI • HONG KONG

Photographs © 2011: iStockphoto: 2 (Susanne Friedrich), 7 (Chris Price), 3 & 8 (Horst Puschmann), 4 (Rudyanto Wijaya); ShutterStock, Inc.: 1 (Anat-oli), cover (mathom), 5 (MilousSK), 6 (Silia Photo).

---

No part of this publication may be reproduced, stored in a retrieval system, or transmitted in any form or by any means, electronic, mechanical, photocopying, recording, or otherwise, without written permission of the publisher. For information regarding permission, write to Scholastic Inc., Attention: Permissions Department, 557 Broadway, New York, NY 10012.

ISBN 978-0-545-34811-9

Cover and interior design by Holly Grundon. Photo research by Veroniqua Quinteros.

Copyright © 2011 by Lefty's Editorial Services. All rights reserved. Published by Scholastic Inc.
SCHOLASTIC, GUIDED SCIENCE READERS, and associated logos are trademarks and/or registered trademarks of Scholastic Inc.

25 24 23 22 21 20 19 18 17        24 25 26/0

Printed in China.        68

It starts with a chicken.

The chicken lays some eggs.

A fluffy chick hatches!

The chick eats and grows.

The chick gets bigger.

The chick becomes a chicken.

The chicken lays some eggs.

GUIDED SCIENCE READERS

www.scholastic.com

ISBN 978-0-545-34811-9

Guided **Science** Readers

# Copycat Critters

**GUIDED SCIENCE READERS™**

# Copycat Critters

### by David Lee

## SCHOLASTIC INC.

NEW YORK • TORONTO • LONDON • AUCKLAND • SYDNEY • MEXICO CITY • NEW DELHI • HONG KONG

Photographs © 2011: Alamy Images: 4 inset (Juniors Bildarchiv), 4 background (Rolf Nussbaumer Photography); Getty Images/Buena Vista Images: cover; iStockphoto: 8 inset (John Carnemolla), 3 inset (Albert Mendelewski), 1 (Kirill Vorobyev); Minden Pictures/Michael Durham; 8 background; Photo Researchers, NY/Nick Garbutt: 3 background; ShutterStock, Inc.: 6 background (creativex), 5 background (Liew Weng Keong), 2 inset (Olga_i), 5 inset (Ingrid Petitjean), 2 background (Studio 37), 6 inset (Johan Swanepoel), 7 inset (Mogens Trolle), 7 background (Rudy Umans).

No part of this publication may be reproduced, stored in a retrieval system, or transmitted in any form or by any means, electronic, mechanical, photocopying, recording, or otherwise, without written permission of the publisher. For information regarding permission, write to Scholastic Inc., Attention: Permissions Department, 557 Broadway, New York, NY 10012.

ISBN 978-0-545-34813-3

Cover and interior design by Holly Grundon. Photo research by Jenna Addesso.

Copyright © 2011 by Lefty's Editorial Services. All rights reserved. Published by Scholastic Inc.
SCHOLASTIC, GUIDED SCIENCE READERS, and associated logos are trademarks and/or registered trademarks of Scholastic Inc.

25 24 23 22 21 20 19 18 17    24 25 26/0

Printed in China.    68

sea horse

horse

This fish looks like a horse.
Hello, copycat!

giraffe

giraffe beetle

This bug looks like a giraffe.
Hello, copycat!

fox

fox squirrel

This squirrel looks like a fox.
Hello, copycat!

This spider looks like a crab.
Hello, copycat!

elephant

elephant seal

This seal looks like an elephant.
Hello, copycat!

zebra

zebra butterfly

This butterfly looks like a zebra.
Hello, copycat!

kangaroo

kangaroo rat

This rat looks like a kangaroo.
Good-bye, copycat!

**GUIDED SCIENCE READERS**

www.scholastic.com

ISBN 978-0-545-34813-3

**GUIDED SCIENCE READERS™**   **D**

# Night Animals

SCHOLASTIC

**GUIDED SCIENCE READERS™**

# Night Animals

### by Alison Kitson

SCHOLASTIC INC.

NEW YORK • TORONTO • LONDON • AUCKLAND • SYDNEY • MEXICO CITY • NEW DELHI • HONG KONG

Photographs © 2011: Alamy Images/Darren Bridges: 5; iStockphoto/Eric Isselée: cover, 1; Media Bakery: 2, 7; Nature Picture Library Ltd./Bence Mate: 3; Photo Researchers, NY: 8 (Hans Reinhard), 6 (B.G. Thomson); ShutterStock, Inc./Yufeng Wang: 4.

No part of this publication may be reproduced, stored in a retrieval system, or transmitted in any form or by any means, electronic, mechanical, photocopying, recording, or otherwise, without written permission of the publisher. For information regarding permission, write to Scholastic Inc., Attention: Permissions Department, 557 Broadway, New York, NY 10012.

ISBN 978-0-545-34812-6

Cover and interior design by Holly Grundon. Photo research by Jenna Addesso.

Copyright © 2011 by Lefty's Editorial Services. All rights reserved. Published by Scholastic Inc.
SCHOLASTIC, GUIDED SCIENCE READERS, and associated logos are trademarks and/or registered trademarks of Scholastic Inc.

25 24 23 22 21 20 19 18 17      24 25 26/0

Printed in China.      68

What happens when you go to sleep?

Night animals wake up!

Raccoons wake up!
They run and play.

Deer wake up!
They eat and drink.

Bats wake up!
They fly and hunt.

What happens when you wake up?

Night animals go to sleep.

**GUIDED SCIENCE READERS**

www.scholastic.com

ISBN 978-0-545-34812-6

**GUIDED SCIENCE READERS**™  **D**

# Tails, Tails, Tails!

**SCHOLASTIC**

**GUIDED SCIENCE READERS**™

# Tails, Tails, Tails!

### by Violet Findley

## SCHOLASTIC INC.

NEW YORK • TORONTO • LONDON • AUCKLAND • SYDNEY • MEXICO CITY • NEW DELHI • HONG KONG

Photographs © 2011: iStockphoto: 7 top right (Sascha Burkard), 2 top left (Malcolm Crooks), cover, 1, 2 top right, 2 bottom, 3 left, 4 top right, 5 top left, 7 middle top, 7 top left, 8 top, 8 bottom left (Eric Isselée), 5 bottom left (Dirk-Jan Mattaar), 7 bottom (Chanyut Sribua-Rawd), 6 left (Vassiliy Vishnevskiy); ShutterStock, Inc.: 4 bottom (Anat-oli), 6 right (Le Do), 3 right (Jaimie Duplass), 5 right (fivespots), 4 top left (Eric Isselée), 8 bottom right (Alexia Khruscheva).

---

No part of this publication may be reproduced, stored in a retrieval system, or transmitted in any form or by any means, electronic, mechanical, photocopying, recording, or otherwise, without written permission of the publisher. For information regarding permission, write to Scholastic Inc., Attention: Permissions Department, 557 Broadway, New York, NY 10012.

ISBN 978-0-545-34814-0

Cover and interior design by Holly Grundon. Photo research by Jenna Addesso.

Copyright © 2011 by Lefty's Editorial Services. All rights reserved. Published by Scholastic Inc.
SCHOLASTIC, GUIDED SCIENCE READERS, and associated logos are trademarks and/or registered trademarks of Scholastic Inc.

25 24 23 22 21 20 19 18 17      24 25 26/0

Printed in China.      68

Tails, tails, tails!

Cats have tails.
Dogs have tails.

Cows and pigs and hens have tails.

Birds have tails and fish have tails.
Snakes have tails with lots of scales.

Deer have itty-bitty tails.
Dragonflies have pretty tails.

Skunks and owls and mice have tails.
Crocs have very scary tails.

Tails, tails, tails!

**GUIDED SCIENCE READERS**

www.scholastic.com

ISBN 978-0-545-34814-0

GUIDED SCIENCE READERS™ **D**

# Who Is Hiding?

SCHOLASTIC

## GUIDED SCIENCE READERS

# Who Is Hiding?

**by Violet Findley**

### SCHOLASTIC INC.

NEW YORK • TORONTO • LONDON • AUCKLAND • SYDNEY • MEXICO CITY • NEW DELHI • HONG KONG

Photographs © 2011: iStockphoto: 2 (Gabriel Bouvigne), 1 (Lusoimages), cover (step2626); Media Bakery: 7, 8; Photo Researchers, NY: 6 (Tom & Pat Leeson), 3 (Rod Planck), 4 (Karl H. Switak); ShutterStock, Inc./M.Moita: 5.

---

No part of this publication may be reproduced, stored in a retrieval system, or transmitted in any form or by any means, electronic, mechanical, photocopying, recording, or otherwise, without written permission of the publisher. For information regarding permission, write to Scholastic Inc., Attention: Permissions Department, 557 Broadway, New York, NY 10012.

ISBN 978-0-545-34809-6

Cover and interior design by Holly Grundon. Photo research by Jenna Addesso.

Copyright © 2011 by Lefty's Editorial Services. All rights reserved. Published by Scholastic Inc.
SCHOLASTIC, GUIDED SCIENCE READERS, and associated logos are trademarks and/or registered trademarks of Scholastic Inc.

25 24 23 22 21 20 19 18 17     24 25 26/0

Printed in China.     68

Who is hiding in the grass?
It's a bug.

Who is hiding in the leaves?
It's a lizard.

Who is hiding in the sand?
It's a snake.

Who is hiding in the water?
It's a frog.

Who is hiding in the snow?
It's a bird.

Who is hiding in the hole?
It's an owl.

Who is hiding behind the tree?
It's just me!

**GUIDED SCIENCE READERS**

www.scholastic.com

ISBN 978-0-545-34809-6

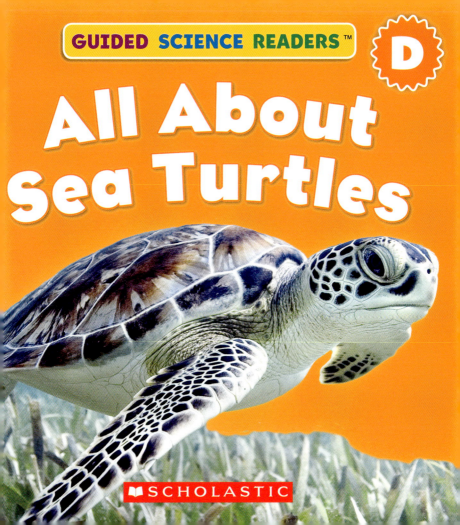

**GUIDED SCIENCE READERS**

# All About Sea Turtles

**by Ben Remington**

SCHOLASTIC INC.

Photographs © 2012: Getty Images: 1 (Michael Gerber), 2 (Monica and Michael Sweet); National Geographic Stock/Steve Winter: 5; Superstock, Inc.: 7 (age fotostock), 6 (Flirt), 8 (NaturePL), cover, 3, 4 (Pacific Stock).

No part of this publication may be reproduced, stored in a retrieval system, or transmitted in any form or by any means, electronic, mechanical, photocopying, recording, or otherwise, without written permission of the publisher. For information regarding permission, write to Scholastic Inc., Attention: Permissions Department, 557 Broadway, New York, NY 10012.

ISBN 978-0-545-49705-3

Cover and interior designed by BHG Graphic Design. Photo research by Liza Charlesworth.

Copyright © 2012 by Lefty's Editorial Services. All rights reserved. Published by Scholastic Inc.
SCHOLASTIC, GUIDED SCIENCE READERS, and associated logos are trademarks and/or registered trademarks of Scholastic Inc.

25 24 23 22 21 20 19 18 17     24 25 26/0
Printed in China.     68

Hello, big sea turtle!

Sea turtles like to swim.

Sea turtles live in the ocean.

But they lay eggs on land.

Crack!
A baby sea turtle is born.

The baby runs to the ocean.
The ocean will be his home.

Good-bye, little sea turtle!

**GUIDED SCIENCE READERS**

www.scholastic.com

ISBN 978-0-545-49705-3

GUIDED SCIENCE READERS™ D

# Hooray for Summer!

SCHOLASTIC

**GUIDED SCIENCE READERS™**

# Hooray for Summer!

**by Lucy Lucero**

## SCHOLASTIC INC.

Photographs © 2012: Getty Images/Frank Siteman/age fotostock: 3; iStockphoto: 5 (Judy Barranco), 1 (luminis); Media Bakery: 4, 7 (Ariel Skelley), 8 (Charlie Edwards), 2 (Jeremy Woodhouse), 6; Shutterstock, Inc./Andrey_Popov: cover.

---

No part of this publication may be reproduced, stored in a retrieval system, or transmitted in any form or by any means, electronic, mechanical, photocopying, recording, or otherwise, without written permission of the publisher. For information regarding permission, write to Scholastic Inc., Attention: Permissions Department, 557 Broadway, New York, NY 10012.

ISBN 978-0-545-49709-1

Cover and interior designed by BHG Graphic Design. Photo research by Liza Charlesworth.

Copyright © 2012 by Lefty's Editorial Services. All rights reserved. Published by Scholastic Inc.
SCHOLASTIC, GUIDED SCIENCE READERS, and associated logos are trademarks and/or registered trademarks of Scholastic Inc.

25 24 23 22 21 20 19 18 17    24 25 26/0
Printed in China.    68

Hooray for summer!
We can ride our bikes.

We can ride our scooters, too.
Zoom, zoom!

Hooray for summer!
We can jump through a sprinkler.

We can jump in a cool pool, too.
Splash, splash!

Hooray for summer!
We can play baseball.

We can play soccer, too.
Kick, kick!

Hooray for summer!
There is so much to do.

**GUIDED SCIENCE READERS**

www.scholastic.com

ISBN 978-0-545-49709-1

Guided Science Readers™

# Lovely Ladybugs

# SCHOLASTIC

**GUIDED SCIENCE READERS**

# Lovely Ladybugs

**by Lydia Carlin**

SCHOLASTIC INC.

Photographs © 2012: Alamy Images: 3 (Juniors Bildarchiv), 8 (Keiji Iwai); iStockphoto: 4 center (Antagain), 4 top (arlindo71), 1 (julichka), 4 background (Marek Mnich), 4 bottom (Steve Snyder); Shutterstock, Inc.: cover (DenisNata), 5 (irin-k); Superstock, Inc.: 7 (Animals Animals), 6 (Juniors), 2 (Minden Pictures).

---

No part of this publication may be reproduced, stored in a retrieval system, or transmitted in any form or by any means, electronic, mechanical, photocopying, recording, or otherwise, without written permission of the publisher. For information regarding permission, write to Scholastic Inc., Attention: Permissions Department, 557 Broadway, New York, NY 10012.

ISBN 978-0-545-49707-7

Cover and interior designed by BHG Graphic Design. Photo research by Liza Charlesworth.

Copyright © 2012 by Lefty's Editorial Services. All rights reserved. Published by Scholastic Inc.
SCHOLASTIC, GUIDED SCIENCE READERS, and associated logos are trademarks and/or registered trademarks of Scholastic Inc.

25 24 23 22 21 20 19 18 17     24 25 26/0
Printed in China.                              68

Want to learn about ladybugs?

Ladybugs have pretty black spots.

Ladybugs are insects.

Ladybugs have six legs.

Ladybugs can crawl.
They can also fly.

Most ladybugs are red.
But some are other colors.

I love ladybugs.
They are lovely!

**GUIDED SCIENCE READERS**

www.scholastic.com

ISBN 978-0-545-49707-7

GUIDED SCIENCE READERS™

D

# Making Ice Cream

SCHOLASTIC

# GUIDED SCIENCE READERS™

# Making Ice Cream

### by Ted Cortese

SCHOLASTIC INC.

Photographs © 2012: Getty Images/Adrian Weinbrecht: 3; iStockphoto: 4 left (Dean Turner), cover (Hakan Dere), 7 left (Uyen Le); Media Bakery: 5 (Daniel Hurst), 8 (JGI), 2 (Kevin Dodge), 6; Shutterstock, Inc.: 4 top right (Danny Smythe), 7 right (Elena Elisseeva), 4 bottom right (Evgeny Karandaev), 1 (Graça Victoria).

No part of this publication may be reproduced, stored in a retrieval system, or transmitted in any form or by any means, electronic, mechanical, photocopying, recording, or otherwise, without written permission of the publisher. For information regarding permission, write to Scholastic Inc., Attention: Permissions Department, 557 Broadway, New York, NY 10012.

ISBN 978-0-545-49706-0

Cover and interior designed by BHG Graphic Design. Photo research by Liza Charlesworth.

Copyright © 2012 by Lefty's Editorial Services. All rights reserved. Published by Scholastic Inc.
SCHOLASTIC, GUIDED SCIENCE READERS, and associated logos are trademarks and/or registered trademarks of Scholastic Inc.

25 24 23 22 21 20 19 18 17     24 25 26/0

Printed in China.      68

I love ice cream!
You love ice cream!

You can buy ice cream.

You can make ice cream, too.
You need cream, sugar, and ice.

You put them in the
ice-cream maker.

Then you turn the crank.

It takes a lot of work
to make ice cream . . .

. . . but it is worth it.

**GUIDED SCIENCE READERS**

www.scholastic.com

ISBN 978-0-545-49706-0

GUIDED **SCIENCE READERS**™

D

# The Super Sun

**Scholastic**

# GUIDED SCIENCE READERS™

# The Super Sun

**by Megan Duhamel**

SCHOLASTIC INC.

Photographs © 2012: Getty Images: 2 (Amanda Tipton Photography), 7 right (Russ Beinder), 8 (Shabbir Ferdous Photography); iStockphoto: cover (Brooke Elizabeth Becker), 1 (s-cphoto); Media Bakery: 7 left (Craig Tuttle), 6 (Roger Harris); Shutterstock, Inc./djgis: 3; Superstock, Inc./Science Faction: 4, 5.

No part of this publication may be reproduced, stored in a retrieval system, or transmitted in any form or by any means, electronic, mechanical, photocopying, recording, or otherwise, without written permission of the publisher. For information regarding permission, write to Scholastic Inc., Attention: Permissions Department, 557 Broadway, New York, NY 10012.

ISBN 978-0-545-49704-6

Cover and interior designed by BHG Graphic Design. Photo research by Liza Charlesworth.

Copyright © 2012 by Lefty's Editorial Services. All rights reserved. Published by Scholastic Inc.
SCHOLASTIC, GUIDED SCIENCE READERS, and associated logos are trademarks and/or registered trademarks of Scholastic Inc.

25 24 23 22 21 20 19 18 17     24 25 26/0

Printed in China.     68

See the sun?

The sun is a star.
It is very big.

The sun is in space.
It is very far away.

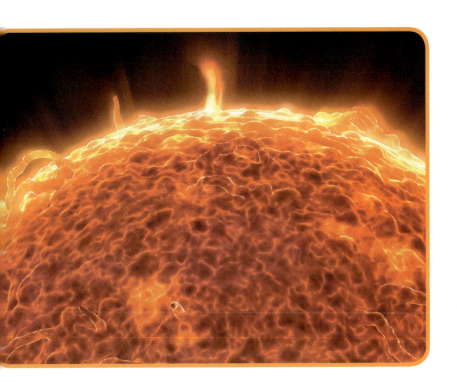

The sun is made of gas.
It is very hot.

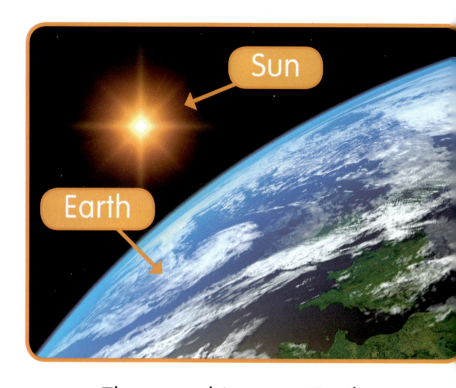

The sun shines on Earth.

The sun shines on plants and animals.

The sun shines on people, too.
The sun is super!

GUIDED SCIENCE READERS

www.scholastic.com

ISBN 978-0-545-49704-6

GUIDED SCIENCE READERS™

**D**

# We Can Go to the Beach

**SCHOLASTIC**

**GUIDED SCIENCE READERS™**

# We Can Go to the Beach

### by Gavin Harper

SCHOLASTIC INC.

Photographs © 2012: Getty Images: 3 (Daniel Hurst Photography), 2 (Mike Timo); iStockphoto: 1 (Chris Leachman), cover (Luis Pedrosa); Media Bakery: 8 (JGI/Jamie Grill), 7 (Paul Burns), 4 (Roy MacMahon), 6 (Tom Merton), 5.

---

No part of this publication may be reproduced, stored in a retrieval system, or transmitted in any form or by any means, electronic, mechanical, photocopying, recording, or otherwise, without written permission of the publisher. For information regarding permission, write to Scholastic Inc., Attention: Permissions Department, 557 Broadway, New York, NY 10012.

ISBN 978-0-545-49708-4

Cover and interior designed by BHG Graphic Design. Photo research by Liza Charlesworth.

Copyright © 2012 by Lefty's Editorial Services. All rights reserved. Published by Scholastic Inc.
SCHOLASTIC, GUIDED SCIENCE READERS, and associated logos are trademarks and/or registered trademarks of Scholastic Inc.

25 24 23 22 21 20 19 18 17      24 25 26/0

Printed in China.      68

Yay!
We can go to the beach today.

We can jump in the waves.
The waves are very cold.

We can look for shells.
The shells are very pretty.

We can build a castle.
The castle is very big.

We can fly a kite.
The kite is very colorful.

We can eat ice cream.
The ice cream is very good.

We can lie in the sun.
The beach is very fun!

**GUIDED SCIENCE READERS**™

www.scholastic.com

ISBN 978-0-545-49708-4

**Guided Science Readers** — D

# Spiders Are Special

SCHOLASTIC

# GUIDED SCIENCE READERS™

# Spiders Are Special

### by Liza Charlesworth

## SCHOLASTIC INC.

NEW YORK • TORONTO • LONDON • AUCKLAND • SYDNEY • MEXICO CITY • NEW DELHI • HONG KONG

Photographs © 2012: Getty Images: 8 (Rundstedt B. Rovillos), 3 (Thomas Shahan); iStockphoto: 5 left (Antagain), 1, 5 right (arlindo71), 4 right (Cristian Baitg), 4 left (Miroslaw Kijewski), cover (Okea); Media Bakery/Philip Bildstein: 6 left; Superstock, Inc.: 7 (All Canada Photos), 6 right (Animals Animals), 2 (Science Faction).

---

No part of this publication may be reproduced, stored in a retrieval system, or transmitted in any form or by any means, electronic, mechanical, photocopying, recording, or otherwise, without written permission of the publisher. For information regarding permission, write to Scholastic Inc., Attention: Permissions Department, 557 Broadway, New York, NY 10012.

ISBN 978-0-545-45978-5

Cover and interior design by Holly Grundon. Photo research by Liza Charlesworth.

Copyright © 2012 by Lefty's Editorial Services. All rights reserved. Published by Scholastic Inc.
SCHOLASTIC, GUIDED SCIENCE READERS, and associated logos are trademarks and/or registered trademarks of Scholastic Inc.

25 24 23 22 21 20 19 18 17      24 25 26/0

Printed in China.      68

Spiders are special!
They have eight legs.

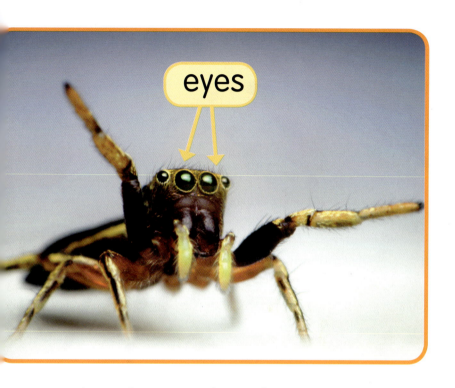

Spiders have a lot of eyes, too.

Spiders can be brown or black.

Spiders can be yellow or green.

Some spiders can hide.
Some spiders can hang.

Some spiders can spin webs.

But all spiders are special!

**GUIDED SCIENCE READERS**

www.scholastic.com

ISBN 978-0-545-45978-5

**GUIDED SCIENCE READERS**

**D**

# "Buzz!" Said the Fuzzy Bee

**SCHOLASTIC**

# "Buzz!" Said the Fuzzy Bee

by Jason Laramie

SCHOLASTIC INC.

NEW YORK • TORONTO • LONDON • AUCKLAND • SYDNEY • MEXICO CITY • NEW DELHI • HONG KONG

Photographs © 2012: Getty Images/Kelly Sillaste: 8; iStockphoto: cover (arlindo71), 1 (Eric Isselée); Media Bakery: 3, 4; Superstock, Inc.: 7 (Animals Animals), 5 (Jerry Shulman), 2 (Minden Pictures), 6 (NaturePL).

No part of this publication may be reproduced, stored in a retrieval system, or transmitted in any form or by any means, electronic, mechanical, photocopying, recording, or otherwise, without written permission of the publisher. For information regarding permission, write to Scholastic Inc., Attention: Permissions Department, 557 Broadway, New York, NY 10012.

ISBN 978-0-545-45977-8

Cover and interior design by Holly Grundon. Photo research by Liza Charlesworth.

Copyright © 2012 by Lefty's Editorial Services. All rights reserved. Published by Scholastic Inc.
SCHOLASTIC, GUIDED SCIENCE READERS, and associated logos are trademarks and/or registered trademarks of Scholastic Inc.

25 24 23 22 21 20 19 18 17    24 25 26/0

Printed in China.    68

"Buzz!" said the fuzzy bee.
Fuzzy bees love spring!

"Tweet!" said the pretty bird.
Pretty birds love spring!

"Meow!" said the playful cat.
Playful cats love spring.

"Woof!" said the lazy dog.
Lazy dogs love spring!

"Ribbit!" said the wet frog.
Wet frogs love spring!

"Squeak!" said the tiny mouse.
Tiny mice love spring!

"Hooray!" said the happy kid.
Happy kids love spring!

GUIDED SCIENCE READERS

www.scholastic.com

Guided Science Readers D

# The Busy Garden

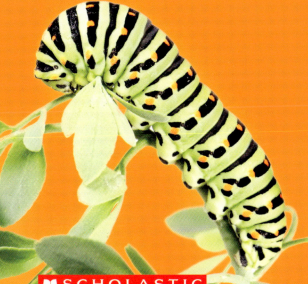

SCHOLASTIC

**GUIDED SCIENCE READERS**™

# The Busy Garden

**by Giovanna Esposito**

SCHOLASTIC INC.

NEW YORK • TORONTO • LONDON • AUCKLAND • SYDNEY • MEXICO CITY • NEW DELHI • HONG KONG

Photographs © 2012: iStockphoto: cover (arlindo71), 8 background (Clifford Shirley), 1 (Gabor Izso), 8 inset (Hakan Dere), 3 (Sarah Holmstrom); Media Bakery: 2 (altrendo images), 7 (Odilon Dimier); Superstock, Inc.: 4 (imagebroker.net), 5, 6 (Minden Pictures).

No part of this publication may be reproduced, stored in a retrieval system, or transmitted in any form or by any means, electronic, mechanical, photocopying, recording, or otherwise, without written permission of the publisher. For information regarding permission, write to Scholastic Inc., Attention: Permissions Department, 557 Broadway, New York, NY 10012.

ISBN 978-0-545-45975-4

Cover and interior design by Holly Grundon. Photo research by Liza Charlesworth.

Copyright © 2012 by Lefty's Editorial Services. All rights reserved. Published by Scholastic Inc.
SCHOLASTIC, GUIDED SCIENCE READERS, and associated logos are trademarks and/or registered trademarks of Scholastic Inc.

25 24 23 22 21 20 19 18 17          24 25 26/0

Printed in China.          68

There is a lot going on in the busy garden. Come and see!

A caterpillar creeps
in the busy garden.
Creep, creep, creep!

A ladybug flies
in the busy garden.
Fly, fly, fly!

A grasshopper hops
in the busy garden.
Hop, hop, hop!

A butterfly flutters
in the busy garden.
Flutter, flutter, flutter!

A spider spins
in the busy garden.
Spin, spin, spin!

A cat dreams
in the busy garden.
Dream, dream, dream!

GUIDED SCIENCE READERS

www.scholastic.com

ISBN 978-0-545-45975-4

**GUIDED SCIENCE READERS**

**D**

# Ants Work Together

**GUIDED SCIENCE READERS™**

# Ants Work Together

## by Violet Findley

SCHOLASTIC INC.

NEW YORK • TORONTO • LONDON • AUCKLAND • SYDNEY • MEXICO CITY • NEW DELHI • HONG KONG

Photographs © 2012: Getty Images: 1 (Kevin Summers), cover (Tim Flach); iStockphoto: 8 (Andrey Pavlov), 3 foreground (Floortje), 5 foreground (klenger), 7 foreground (pagadesign), 6 (Sandra Henderson); Superstock, Inc.: 4, 5 (Bill Gozansky/age fotostock), 2, 3 (Minden Pictures), 7 background (Wolfgang Kaehler).

No part of this publication may be reproduced, stored in a retrieval system, or transmitted in any form or by any means, electronic, mechanical, photocopying, recording, or otherwise, without written permission of the publisher. For information regarding permission, write to Scholastic Inc., Attention: Permissions Department, 557 Broadway, New York, NY 10012.

ISBN 978-0-545-45976-1

Cover and interior design by Holly Grundon. Photo research by Liza Charlesworth.

Copyright © 2012 by Lefty's Editorial Services. All rights reserved. Published by Scholastic Inc.
SCHOLASTIC, GUIDED SCIENCE READERS, and associated logos are trademarks and/or registered trademarks of Scholastic Inc.

25 24 23 22 21 20 19 18 17     24 25 26/0

Printed in China.     68

Ants work together to cut big leaves.

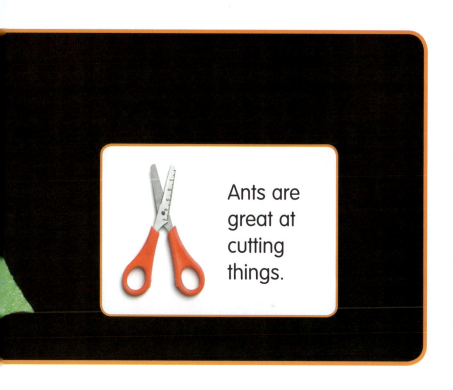

Ants are great at cutting things.

They use teamwork!

Ants work together
to carry big leaves.

Ants are great at lifting things.

They use teamwork!

Ants work together
to build big homes.

Ants are great at building things.

They use teamwork!

Ants work together
to get big jobs done.
They use teamwork!

GUIDED SCIENCE READERS

ISBN 978-0-545-45976-1